Homeless on the Range

Life on the road in a Model A Ford
during the Great Depression

by Barbara Barden Margerum

San Leandro Press
Santa Barbara, California

email: barbaramargerum@cox.net

ISBN 1442164638
EAN-13 9781442164635

HOMELESS ON THE RANGE

You might think it strange
That our "home on the range"

Was a Model A Ford...all black
Mom and Dad in front, me in the back

It easily slept three
Mom, Dad and me

The jobs welding pipe
Turned out to be hype

So we took to the road
Our car our abode

Day after day, week after week
Through a landscape often bleak

Past telephone lines
And Burma Shave signs

Looking for work...young, strong
We joined an ever growing throng

That would head West and find jobs
Defy the grim words of Hobbes

Then, lo, somewhere along the way
We learned in this striving day by day

That not being gainfully employed
Was actually something to be enjoyed.

We made a great trio
Sang songs with brio

We always had enough to eat
Kept ourselves clean and neat

Yes, the jobs were menial....alas
Just enough for food and gas

Did this experience help me shoulder
Vicissitudes as I grew older?

Well, yes
I guess.

HOMELESS ON THE RANGE

This is the story of my family's odyssey during the darkest days of the Depression, a time when one fourth of the nation's work force was unemployed, when farmers not only lost their farms, but their topsoil as the most severe drought in decades spread across the Great Plains and turned much our productive land into a giant Dust Bowl. From 1929 to 1933 unemployment soared from 3.2% to 24.9% Banks failed, and people's savings of a lifetime were wiped out.

We hear about the stock market crash of 1929, and "Black Tuesday", but in truth the depression reached its depth in 1932 and 1933. From 1930 through 1933 industrial stocks lost 80% of their value.

Long Letters

Bleak statistics, but to a young couple, Hugh Halstead Barden and Ruth Andres Barden and their four year old daughter, Barbara they were the realities of a day to day struggle to live. Their saga comes to life in the long detailed letters my mother, Ruth, wrote to her sister Thelma Andres Rennels, during our search for survival in our Model A Ford. After my mother died my Aunt Thelma's son, Ray, sent me the letters. They don't tell me everything. I still have many unanswered questions about how they coped, but, they are a rich reservoir of our life for a short period, and I quote them generously in telling my tale of homeless on the range.

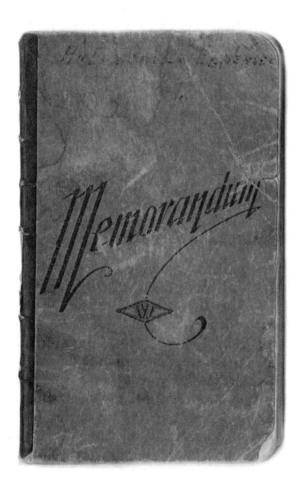

My Dad's Daily Journal

The letters are supplemented by a little notebook my father kept with day-to-day expenses, mileage, work, and pitiful hourly wages earned.

One of my greatest regrets is not reaching out to my mother while she was alive for her stories and memories of these times:

TOO LATE

Who to ask, has keys to the past
No one is left, I am the last

So many questions, so many gaps
I had the chance, I let it lapse

Mother forgive me, your stories of old
Now lost forever, will never be told

Mother's voice rings out so clearly in these letters, that now at least one story can be told. Seven years after my mother's death in 2002 at the age of 96, this is my effort to recapture the time they packed up their car, their daughter, their few belongings and left family and friends for the West, seeking a new life.

Was a Model A Ford...all black
Mom and Dad in front, me in the back

After a brief period of working as a welder in Red Oak, Iowa and Steubenville, Ohio my folks headed back to their base in St. Louis, Missouri, visiting Mother's parents in Illinois en route. Then we left St. Louis on Tuesday, March 31, 1931. Dad's little journal noted they left at 9:45 a.m. and that the trusty Model A Ford's odometer read 12,489. I had just turned four. In her first long and detailed letter to sister Thelma, Mother writes that they...

...bought a gasoline auto-cook kit stove, 2 burner, and a four party set of aluminum dishes, each pan fits into the other. They're both in the Sears-Roebuck catalog.

We got into Springfield, Mo at 5:30 and went up through town and got groceries. Rented a cabin out on the edge of town for $1. Had a laundry stove in it so didn't use our stove. We used our dishes tho and they sure are keen.

There wasn't much excitement in the long and sparse landscape, so such anecdotes as this formed the drama of the day:

We followed a car for quite a way and the little boy in the back seat kept smiling and waving at Barbara. When they turned off on another road Barbara waved goodbye to him and said, 'I believe that boy was flirting with me'

Past telephone lines
And Burma Shave signs

No radio, no reading material, no games, very little unique in the scenery. The Burma Shave signs and the racing with the freight trains relieved the tedium of the acres of sand and sage.

Are your whiskers
When you wake
Tougher than
A two-bit steak

Uncle Rube
Buys tube
One week
Looks sleek

We left Springfield the next morning at 8:30. I fixed something for our lunch so we didn't have to stop long. I drove for about an hour or so but the roads were so rough— no pavement and Hugh kept fussing at me so I never drove anymore. We went through a corner of Kansas and then into Oklahoma. We had a flat tire when we got up the next morning. A little nail caused it. Hugh fixed tire and we went down town to see about pipelines but none was started yet.

*Friday we got up and went into Okla. City and
found out about work, there was nothing doing. Saw state
capitol building. Very pretty. Left there at 11:30..had
Milky Ways for dinner. Roads were terribly rough and the
wind was blowing so hard and the sand was flying every
way. Saw the remains of snow drifts 95 mi. out of Okla.
City. And then shortly afterwards we had to detour and
OH!,the mud. There had been four feet of snow drifts in
the road and the mud was terrible. We were in one mud
hole over the running board but the old Ford rocked out.
The mud here is red. There was 25 miles of that mud.*

Inquiries about welding jobs on the pipelines, rumored to be
ubiquitous, proved again and again to be just that…rumors.
We chased the myth from town to town. Many mornings my
dad woke up to yet another flat tire. Patching the inner tube
was a ritual performed over and over.

*Begin to see sage brush and also saw several dead
cows lying out on the ranches about covered with sand. I
kept watching for cowboys and finally saw 3 of them
gallop out of a little town we went thru. We got into
Amarillo, Texas at 1:30 mountain time and we got Easter
eggs for Barbara. Hugh went to see about pipeline, but
nothing started yet, so we decided to go to El Paso.*

Easter Sunday. I got up and fixed Barbara a nest and put the eggs in it and she was so surprised when she woke up. She couldn't eat her candy tho, for she'd been vomiting in the night and ever since she got up. Hugh and I ate her candy eggs.

<u>Easter Sunday on the Road</u>

We saw our first snow-capped mountains....a short drive out of Roswell, New Mexico, and found out later they were 350 miles away. One sure can see far in this country. We stopped in a little valley and ate lunch and some boy asked us for a ride to a ball game. We also picked up a Mexican boy and let them both hang on. [I guess that means they stood on the running board] The boy told us a lot about the country and the mountains and named a lot of the plants on the desert.

We began to get in the mountains then and we went up to 8040 feet. The top was a forest of pine trees...very very tall trees...they sure were pretty. At the foot of the mountains we went thru the Apache Indian reservation. My! Those Indians do live in old ramshackled huts and wigwams and tents. Sure looks dirty around there. They are almost as black as Negroes.

We began to see another range of mts. In the distance and they looked as if they were in water (we thought at first it was a mirage) so the next town we came to (towns are few and far between) we asked about the mts and what we thought was water and the man told us 'twas white sand and 'twas 75 miles away. The white sand are a natural phenomenon.

Mountains

A Brief Mexican Adventure

Had breakfast and went in to town (El Paso) to find out about work. They told us about a pipeline in Deming, New Mexico. We were right on the Mexican border..the Rio Grande River dividing Texas and Mexico, so we parked and walked over to Juarez. Our car would have had to be searched if we rode over. Bridge toll was 2 cents each. As soon as we got across the bridge women, men and boys began begging. Boys with a block of wood and a box of polish would beg to shine your shoes. Hugh let one of the kids shine his shoes. Cost one cent, so Hugh gave him a nickel... Every door is a saloon…went in a couple and Hugh got a beer and I got soda. We saw 2 men put in jail. The police there carry shot guns. Bought our cards and stamps in a curio shop and saw some dressed fleas, dressed as bride and groom. There are some right pretty girls…ones not so dark. The married Mexican women wear black shawls over their heads and the single girls go bareheaded.

The jobs welding pipe
Turned out to be hype

The pipeline had left Deming so we went on to Lordsburg. The line had moved from there.

We crossed the Continental Divide in the afternoon, that is where the water flows to the Atlantic Ocean on one side and the Pacific on the other.

We crossed the state line into Arizona at Rodeo and had to stop at a quarantine station and be searched. We had a dozen oranges that we'd bought the night before and we could not take them into Arizona, so we ate them there at the station with the help of three other people in another car. We went on to the pipeline and 'twas a big job, but they had all their own help from Wisconsin and wouldn't take on an outsider. They told us of a line in Douglas, Arizona so we started there. Got there but they didn't need anyone and was finished all but 10 miles. Douglas is on the Mexican border too so we went to Mexico again. Just a fence for the border line. We parked and walked over. As we came back the custom officer ask me for my card! Hugh had to tell him I was his wife. I was sure peeved.

Years later Mother still told this story and of how humiliated she was to be taken for a Mexican. With her jet black hair and her olive skin beginning to darken with the desert sun, she no longer looked liked the young woman from Missouri.

On to Bisbee and Tombstone, Arizona

We left Douglas and the next town we came thru was Bisbee-it's a mile town—a mile above sea level. The houses are built right on the mt. Sides. Looks like they are just hanging in space. Everything is pretty and green there tho and the roses were just beautiful. Bisbee is a copper and lead mining town. We left Bisbee and went almost straight up to over 6000 ft. in less than a mile and then right back down again.

Another interesting town we went thru was Tombstone, Ariz. It was such a town as Zane Grey writes about. A real tough town. We went out to Boot-Hill graveyard. Named that because most of the men there boots on—shot down on sight. The mounds are heaps of rocks piled up to resemble a grave. There's about 300 to 400 graves there. Hugh said they piled the rocks up like that so the coyotes wouldn't dig up the graves.

We stopped at a filling station and asked about the town and the town is kept as much like it used to be as possible. At one time there were 61 saloons in town —17 of them in one block. No decent woman would walk along that side of the street. They have a "Helldorado" there every year. The men all let their whiskers grow and the women dress as they would 50 or 60 years ago. They have parades and pageants— covered wagons—Indians and oh, everything as near as they can as it used to be. This year its held Oct 9-10-11 and 12. From 20,000 to 30,000 people come there to see it. Sure is a hot town then.

Their saga is a wonderful combination of job-seeker and tourist. They were always curious about the new and wonderful things they were encountering and Mother was tireless in her descriptions and explanations to sister, Thelma.

Road Rescue

We went on to Tuscon. Sure is pretty city. Lots of palm trees. We were stopped at another quarantine station just out of Tuscon but he didn't bother us as we had our sticker on the windshield from the last station. Left Tuscon about 6:00 to go to next town and found out it was 63 miles away. 17 miles out of town we ran into cattle in the road and a car over on its side in the ditch. He had hit a cow and turned over. It had just happened a few minutes before we got there. Three men in the car—one that his kneecap was broken—never hurt the others. We took the injured man and one of the others to a filling station 1/2 mi. away. They were lucky to find a wrecker there. Twas getting dark before we left there and twas nothing but desert all the way. Twas pitch dark and the lights would shine on those giant cactus and twas kinda scary.

We got to Florence at 8:30 and hadn't had any supper. There was a wood stove in the cabin and twas so hot we didn't want to start a fire so decided we'd use our stove for the 1st time. Guess we didn't kno how to operate it cause we tried until 10:00 to get it going and gave up and ate a piece of cake and went to bed hungry.

Yes, the jobs were menial... alas
Just enough for food and gas

In Mesa, Arizona they found a couple they had known in St. Louis...Audrey and Fred Kopeski and their son, Donald, who was about my age. Having temporarily given up on the welding jobs, my dad joined Fred in working in the citrus orchards...tough work, digging holes for new trees. As his little journal recorded:

Thursday, April 9, 14,426 mi. Went out with Fred and got job but had to come in and borrow a shovel. Dug holes

to set out orange trees and finished at noon. 5 hrs. for $ $1.25. Rode around some in afternoon. Bought straw hat 29 cents and groceries $1.19. Cabin 50 cents. Gas and jug 43 cents. Totals made $1.25 spent $2.41. Things, ... vegetables, etc. are sure cheap here. Gasoline is 19 and 20 cents a gallon. Twenty-five and 30 cents an hour is all that is paid.

Mother's long letter then outlines an elaborate design for how Uncle John and Aunt Thelma could convert an old car they had on the farm:

John, if you kids intend to start out one of these days, why don't you take the wheels of that old car in your barn lot and build you a trailer and build a house right on the trailer, say a 9 by 10 or what ever size you want. Have it wide enuf at the back so your day-bed would fit in the end. Use your card table with oil cloth over it for your eating table. Get a folding camp stove. Build shelves along the sides of the house for placing things… utensils and clothes, etc. Use boxes or get folding camp chairs—and you have lamp and lantern, irons, tub and washboard and all your utensils and you kids would be setting pretty. Use your 2 gal. cream can to carry water in. Say! You kids <u>would be</u> setting pretty. Wish we had something like that.

It shouldn't cost so much to build a house like that. Your tires and license and lumber would be about all the expense and you've several months to think about it in. You could store your furniture in the back bedroom and lock it up. 'Twould be worth it just to live in when you go to see Les Rennels, wouldn't it? These are merely suggestions.

Dad's little 3½ x 6 inch daily journal continues to record the mileage on the Model A and every penny earned and every penny spent, including frequent expenditures of "cig. papers 5 cents." In addition to the fruit picking and planting he did some auto repair for a guy named Carpenter. "Helped monkey with Carpenter's car and got a loaf of bread for it."

As the constant hope for pipeline jobs began to fade he and Fred Kopeski worked planting citrus trees and soon the work narrative began to include the two women...Ruth and Audrey. Mother never mentions in her letters what arrangement they made for the two 4 year olds, but as Dad's careful journal began to record:

> *The girls picked apricots all day and got 36 lugs all told. We worked until 2 a.m." "Ruth, Fred and I picks cots from 9:30 to 12 and we all picked all afternoon til 6:30, got 48 lugs.*

Bad News from Back Home

Finally, in early May Mother got a letter about her Mother's lingering illness. She had left for the trip west knowing that her both her Mother and Father were not well, but she thought they were getting better. In an anguished appeal to Thelma she writes:

Your letter set me to worrying again. I thought Mamma was getting better. Dessie [Mother's much younger sister] has just written me two letters—1st one she told me the folks were home and Mamma was awful sick and the 2nd one she said Mamma was so much better and I haven't heard anything since so I supposed she was better. She had been in bed 2 weeks then but now she's been in bed about 5 weeks. Please ans these questions. Can't Mamma even sit up? Does she go out of her head like she did at first? If the disease is from eating rare pork can it be cured? Is Poppa in bed too? Does he have the same symptoms as Mamma. Is Mamma's side swollen like Pop's neck? I wish I was there. Gosh! You don't know how worried I am. Will you send me back a letter by air mail so I'll get it real soon. Just put a nickel in the box or 5 cents worth of stamps on the letter and write AIR MAIL across it. I would never have gone if I'd thot that all this would happen. Seems like everything was going along so smoothly when we left and now all this! I'll always let you know where we are so you can get word to us, but if I thot Mamma wouldn't get any better I'd try and get home. Its so terribly hot here. I don't see how the boys work out in this hot sun. Ans. right away Thelma and let me know about Mama and Papa. I'm depending on you.

After several weeks of hard work planting citrus, staking small trees and picking apricots in the Mesa area the fruit picking season drew to an end and Dad reports:

> *May 19, Spent in Mesa $91.37 Made $77.52*

Traveling with the Kopeskis they made their way to Yuma and El Centro, the Imperial Valley, past the Salton Sea and on to Beaumont, California to see about cherry picking jobs.

> *Friday, May 22, 15420 miles, Went all around through the valley but no chance of a job. Fellow told us about jobs in onions at Coachella so we left about noon to go back. Got a job from a Mex and camped on his place. $1.09*
> *Saturday, May 23, 15,500. Got up at 4:30 and went to work at 5:00. Audrey went with us in the A.M. and Ruth in the P.M. Worked 10 hr. and made $1.12 apiece. That was the end of the onions. Out of Indio we ran into a regular gale and Fred ran out of gas bucking it. Had to go on and bring gas back to Fred and some time during the excitement I lost two $1 bills.*

They went on to San Bernardino and Los Angeles, stopping at the Santa Monica Beach. They drove north to San Fernando and Saugus and then back to the coast.

Drove til 9:00 P.M. and stopped at Santa Barbara County free camp. Sure a nice place.

Then on up the coast to Livermore and San Jose with occasional jobs in the walnut groves.

Went up to Jenny Lind on the Calveras River. Found fine swimming hole and went in. Got 6 gal gas, 45 cents, and qt oil 10 cents 40 cents of groc. Spent 95 cents.

MAMMA DIES- June 4, 1931

A telegram with news of mamma's death was sent to General Delivery in Byron, California. Mother says in her letter to Thelma:

> *And whoever sent the telegram sent it General Delivery, it went to the P.O. Hugh asked for the mail there Fri. morn but guess the telegram came in after that. So I asked Sat. morn and there the telegram was. Then it was too late to even think of coming and I thot I'd go crazy. When was Mama buried and where? You kno the last time I saw Mama was just before her birthday and she cried so when we left. Oh! I wish we hadn't come out here. Thelma, I can't write anymore. My heart is just bursting. It seems there is nothing I can do to forget.*

I do remember my Mother and Dad calling back to Illinois, sobbing and supporting one another. Mother closes her tearful letter with this:

> *Barbara doesn't realize Mama is gone. Poor little dear she is so loving and sympathetic to me and so is Hugh.*

I certainly didn't know what was happening. No one told me, but I knew it was not good.

Family Reports on Mamma's Death

Thelma wrote a 10 page letter describing Mamma's last days and her funeral:

> "For the last 2 wks before Mamma died she would get so nervous and scared when the doctor came for fear he was going to lance her again."

Thelma writes that on June 2 (two days before she died):

> "...she went to sleep about 4 and when she woke up she couldn't speak out loud, not even whisper. It scared her so that her heart went bad and is was about an hour before her voice came back....she couldn't speak very loud and from then on she seemed to be in a stupor, yet she knew everyone. Mamma didn't suffer much from then on because she was so awfully weak. She just spit up bloody looking stuff nearly all the time. Helen and I sat with her most of the nite and just as fast as we could unroll toilet paper she spit it full. She didn't have to cough at all for it to come. Just seemed like she'd clear her throat the least bit and she'd have a whole mouthful. It was so terrible and pitiful to have to see Mamma suffer they way she did those 9 weeks. You may be thankful Ruth that you didn't see her in a way. But, I do wish you could have seen her when she was lying in the casket. She just looked beautiful. One couldn't tell that she had ever suffered to look at her face. There isn't much more to tell you, only how easy it seemed for her to die. Just slept away. Oh, Ruth, I think the same as you do, I too

am sure going to try and do better from now on and live to see Mamma in Heaven some day. It's all we can do now.

I've sat here and wrote till my fire is out and I'll have to start it and get my dishes and the separator washed. Ray is fine. He never forgets you kids. I'll bet he'd be tickled to see you Barbara. Every time he sits on the little chamber he thinks of you, Barbara and he nearly always says, 'Barbara grunts this way.'"

Cheer Up

"Now Ruth I want you to cheer up and take interest and eat some for you know that we have one wonderful blessing ahead of us to think of, and that is, that we know that Mamma is in Heaven. Isn't that something dear to think of. And don't feel that we should be downhearted, unhappy and mourn when we got all that to think about. It's hard to think that we have given her up forever but we still have that wonderful thought that she is in Heaven. So Cheer Up!

Did Dessie (Mother's younger sister) tell you how terribly it was storming at the time of Mamma's death? It just blew and the lightning was awful and poured down rain."

Thelma enclosed a now yellowed newspaper clipping with the headline, <u>Wife of Russell Newell is Killed by Lightning</u>. It describes the death by lightning of 32 year old Mabel Replogle Newell on Thursday evening about 5:30. According to the news report of Mamma's death headlined, <u>Mrs. W. E. Andres Dies in Her Home</u> Mamma died that evening at 6:10.

MRS. W. E. ANDRES DIES IN HER HOME

Mrs. Alma Dora Louthan Andres, aged 56 years, wife of William E. Andres, died in the family residence, 1436 Tenth street, at 6:10 o'clock on Thursday evening after a ten weeks' illness.

Funeral services will be conducted in the First United Brethren church of Charleston at 2 o'clock on Sunday afternoon by the Reverend Harvey E. Edwards of Casey. Burial will be in Mound cemetery.

Mrs. Andres was converted and joined the Unity Chapel church. She was a faithful member and was loved by all who knew her.

Her husband, the following children are left: Mrs. William H. (Mary) Leitch, Charleston; George Andres, Charleston; Robert Andres, Decatur; T. K. Andres, St. Louis, Mo.; Mrs. Hugh (Ruth) Borden, Byron, Cal.; Mrs. John (Thelma) Rennels, Charleston; and Dessie, Clarence and Virginia, at home. She also leaves three brothers, four sisters, and fifteen grandchildren. Her youngest sister, Mrs. Clara Blasdell, of Grand Chain, Ill., was at her bedside when Mrs. Andres passed away.

Mother also got letters from her sister-in-law, Helen (Dad's sister who married Mother's brother, Ted). She offered this simple condolence in her letter:

"Honey, I know there isn't any real consolation to offer you, but just remember that she had suffered so much that she couldn't stay without being in agony all the time. And she went to easily, she seemed to just be going to sleep."

Her oldest sister, Mary, wrote too.

"Dear Little Sister: I read the letter you had written to the folks last night. Oh, Ruth you'll never know how much Mamma suffered.

It was terrible. She was in a serious condition all alone. There was times when we thot she might be getting better.

Oh, Ruth we'll always miss her. But Ruth she was prepared to go and we must live so we can meet her in Heaven. Haven't any more time. Cheer up and think everything was for the best. With love, Mary."

Life and the Search for Work Goes On

The day after they got the telegram telling them of Mamma's death they went on San Francisco and Dad's daily journal describes their time in San Francisco, Oakland, San Mateo and Hayward in a few sentences:

Drove around town sight-seeing and down to the beach. Went to Chinatown. Stopped and watched the Hayward Rodeo for a while." Went to Oakland to see about pipeline but no luck. Went across San Mateo bridge, 7 1/10 mi. long to South Frisco, but no job there. Drove along Skyline Blvd. And saw some wonderful scenery. Got into clouds on Kings Mt. Saw Methusalah Redwood tree and Woodside store (1854).

For the next few days his daily notes describe Ruth and Aud and their cutting 'cots around Tracy, CA "Ruth and Aud went to work at noon cutting for another Houston and cut 4 boxes @ 12 cents this afternoon. Made $1.35" Day after day... listing the number of boxes, and the meager wages.

But, it wasn't all work. "Went to Tracy and got a dress for Ruth. Went to Apricot Festival and saw wrestling and boxing and took kids on merry-go-round and little autos."

More Bad News

"Saturday, July 4. Got telegram" That was the announcement of Dad's father's death. More tears, but no explanation to me about why the sadness. I never knew Dad's father. His mother had died when Dad was 11 or 12 and his older sister, Mary raised him in Baden, which is part of St. Louis. He was not close to his dad, but still his death had my dad sobbing.

The next fruit-picking was pears around Modesto, CA. It meant 10 hour days and very little money.

Sunday, July 12. 17,272 on the Model A. Got oil and gas in Stockton. Saw State Capitol in Sacramento. Very pretty town. Drove til 8:45 and stopped right in the heart of the mts. Sure a pretty place.

July 13 17,438. Got to Donner Lake which is very pretty and at which the Donner party camped in 1846-47. Very tragic story. Drove over to Lake Tahoe. Stopped in Reno for awhile and saw the Washoe County Court house. Went into a gambling club and won a dollar but then lost it another game and 25 cents besides. Had a puncture coming across Carson Sink. What a place for a puncture. Got gas and oil in Lovelock and then about 4 mi. out had another flat. Fixed tire while Ruth got supper and then drove on past Winnemucca. Went to bed out on the desert at 12:00 midnight.

The highlight of the next leg of the trip was near Elko, NV where "just after dark we saw a very brilliant meteor fall. To us it looked to be about the size of an indoor ball and for a part of it's fall it had a tail between 1 to 2 yards long. It broke into several pieces and finally burned itself out."

We made a great trio
Sang songs with brio

On the long, long stretches of what was often barren land with few signs of life, my Dad raised his voice in song. Mother and I joined in and I remember those moments fondly. I don't think, despite the meager variety of the days, that I was ever bored. Maybe I was and didn't know it, but the singing certainly helped. My favorites were, <u>Swing Low, Sweet Chariot</u> (it still is), <u>Buffalo Gals</u>, <u>Big Rock Candy Mountain</u>, <u>Oh, Dem Golden Slippers</u>, and <u>So Long Oo-long, How Long You Gonna be Gone</u>, a wonderful song I thought my Dad had made up. Years later I looked this last one up and discovered it was a hit of the 1920's. I'm including the words to some of these "classics" at the end of this little memoir in case you want to sing while driving instead of listening to book tapes, watching TV and DVDs, playing video games, listening to NPR, learning French, talking on your phone, or any one of the latest diversions that keep you and your children from being bored.

Finally in August Mother began writing again to sister Thelma with this introduction:

> *I kno you think I'm terrible for not answering your letter but I just haven't felt like it... also you've wondered where we are and what we're doing.*
>
> *Its so hard to write home to you kids for it brings thots of Mama and I just can't let myself think about it all. I get so blue and homesick and oh so dissatisfied that I can hardly stand it. I kno you don't understand how I feel and I can't explain in a letter. I'll try tho from now on to keep in touch with you often.*
>
> *On July 12 we left Byron to go to Butte, Montana. We went up in the northern part of California and nearly across the state of Nevada and then into Idaho and then in Montana. There was about 5 pipe line jobs there and we were in Butte, Deer Lodge, Helena, and Wolf Creek and Hugh couldn't get on a single one of them. He was so sure he could so he was down right disappointed."*
>
> *We talked over what we would do then so I suggested we come over thru the northern part of Idaho, into Washington, Oregon and back into Calif. So we did. No work all the way.*
>
> *Then they got to Turlock and the peach season. Hugh lifting trays and me cutting them. We stayed in Turlock a wk. And worked 2 half days. Hugh got disgusted and he despised the work in fruit too so we packed up and left for Los Angeles.*

It easily slept three
Mom, Dad and me

I noticed random references in Dad's little daily journal that intrigued me...all were about "the platform."

Wednesday, April 22 Spent 45 cents for lumber and made platform.

Friday, April 24 Got bolt for platform 10 cents

Friday, May 8 Went to town in A.M. and got 27 cents groc. And 15 cents paint for platform

Monday, May 18. No work today Bot Ruth and B. hats 30 cents, candy 10 cents, meat 15 cents mattress $1.75 jars, 19 cents nails 5 cents and bread 10 cents. Looked all over for bed but couldn't find one to suit. Spent $2.63.

All these "platform" references became clear in Mother's explanation to Thelma detailing how we lived on the road. After we got to California she wrote in her letter of August 1931:

Now I'll tell you something about our trip. I must tell you how we travel. We didn't spend any money only for eats and gas and oil. We have a platform on the back of the car and we pack 2 suitcases and 2 cardboard boxes on it and then on the inside we have a box of fruit (I got cans and

---

canned several quarts of fruit as we went along) and a box of groceries that come up even with the back seat. We also carry our camp stove and dishes inside. We have our bedclothes and pillows and we bought a daybed pad for $1.75 in Mesa. We also carry one suitcase inside with things we need to change as we go along. When night comes we take the dishes, stove and suitcase out and turn down the 2 front seats and spread the mattress out and we sure have got a keen bed. It really is comfortable. Barbara sleeps by the wheel and me in the middle and Hugh gets the long side...you kno so he can have room for his big feet. Ha. We roll the windows down and it sure is cool. (We have to keep them up if there's mosquitoes but we didn't run into them at all.) We were either in mts. or desert all time and they don't breed there.

We always had enough to eat
Kept ourselves clean and neat

About our meals. We can camp most any place because we have a gallon jug and we carry water in it so we don't have to worry about camping some place where there's water. We also have a running board ice box and we carry groceries like pot., sugar, salt and bread, milk, butter and canned goods that we'll use each meal, in the icebox so we don't have to open up the big groc. box inside...that's full of reserve groceries.

It takes us about an hour to get started of a morn. For we have to get breakfast and wash dishes and wash and comb and change clothes if they're dirty and also make up the bed.

That not being gainfully employed
Was actually something to be enjoyed

Lots of times it takes longer because we'd explore places we'd stop. One morn when we were eating breakfast in a National Forest we saw a deer (she sure was pretty) about 50 ft. from us, stopped and looking all around, so alert. She spied us and she leaped off into the woods in a flash. We all got a real good look at her tho. She had been down to the river for a drink. We saw so many places thru the forests where fires had been and saw several fires in the distance.

In the Mts. in Montana it is beautiful. We drove in canyons for miles...the canyon just wide enuf for a railroad track, a creek bed and the highway and the road wound just like this   and the sides were just straight up. Surely was pretty. Washington is nothing but yellow wheat fields on big hills. They use combines to cut the wheat and we counted from 16 to 38 horses on each combine.The hills are too steep to use tractors. Of all the pretty, most beautiful scenic country we were thru was Oregon.

Photo Courtesy National Geographic Society

Dad's journal describes seeing the Indians on the Columbia River with long handled dip nets. He expands with this:

> *Drove on thru The Dalles and saw wonderful scenery all the way to Hood River. Went up to Cloud Cap Inn way up on the slope of Mt. Hood and from there walked about a mile up to a glacier and ate some glacier ice.*

*We came all the way to Portland and there was
something of interest or beauty every mile of the
way. The Columbia River is so pretty. Spokane,
Wash. is a pretty city. We have several pictures we
took....haven't developed them yet."*

*Idaho is mostly farming where we went thru. We
saw Twin Falls and Shoshone Falls tho in Idaho and
that was very pretty. About Nevada... we were in
Reno about an hour or so. Gambling is wide open
in Nevada and Reno is all gambling houses. Hugh
was in one of the houses and won $1 and then lost it
so we left. I would have gone in too but I just had on
a house dress and no stockings so I stayed in the car,
but I walked past and looked in several of them.
From Reno on across Nevada there's nothing but
desert and oh, how hot... 'twas over 120 degrees.*

The journey down through California was a series of small
jobs picking fruit for a meager wages, constantly having to
repair punctures on the diminishing stock of inner tubes and at
20,400 miles on the old Ford, a major overhaul. Here's how
Dad described it on July 31:

*Went to Modesto and got some grinding compound,
valve lifter and grinder. Ground valves and took pan
off. Will put in new rings tomorrow. Bot 2 new valves,
new set of rings and 40 cents worth of gaskets.*

> *Also took cracked manifold to welder. Finished repairing car and it runs like a clock. Ruth helped a lot. Cost 87 cents tools, 30 cents compound, 20 cents shellac, 75 cents welding and $2.90 for parts.*

Imagine a valve job for a total cost of $5.02! Keeping the Ford running was a major concern. An earlier repair was described by him this way:

> *Left at 8:10 after having to crank car twice. Starter wouldn't respond. Stopped to get gas and had to be towed to get started. Went a couple of miles and engine stalled and had to be towed again. Stopped again but pushed a little to hill and got started down it. Stalled again and after a while got a push and this time kept it running until I got to Dillon to Ford garage. Ground strap on the battery was broken. Got several other little things done and patched a tire that had a slow leak. Got a boot for the tire and oil change.*

The recollection of my Dad patching inner tubes is still one of my most vivid memories of him. Spitting on the suspected puncture to see if it would bubble, carefully scraping that spot with the little metal tool, applying the adhesive from a little tube on to the patch and then tenderly applying it to the treated wound like a band aid to a child's scrape. It never failed to fascinate me, even though the frequency of this ritual must have tested my Dad's equanimity.

His next entry, his last in this tightly packed reservoir of facts, minutiae, impressions, accounting, mileage and daily striving was simply, Sun. Aug 2. I guess they arrived in Los Angeles, because on the next page is a list of four cars, Chrysler Coupe, Essex Red Old, Olds and next to the Chrysler is the date 2/7 and $1.00. This must have been the beginning of his work at the auto repair shop that Mother describes below to Thelma. I don't know what happened to that venture, but I think it too turned out to be another tale of hope and hype.

Mother closes her letter to Thelma with:

Guess this is all about the states. I could write pages more but won't now I could tell you so much better.

How is Johnny Ray? Its swell that he'll have a little sister. Sure was surprised Thelma and I hope it's a little girl.*

*It wasn't. Son Max was born a few months hence and Johnny Ray is Thelma's son, who so wisely saved these letters.

And as a final report from Los Angeles where they hoped to settle for a while:

Hugh settled a deal today. He's a partner in an auto repair and painting shop and he starts to work in the morn. He thinks he'll like it fine. He has to now since he's invested in it.

Where on earth they had to money to "invest" is still a mystery to me and one of the many unanswered questions I encountered in trying to write this saga.

Mother's firsthand report from Hollywood Land:

This morn we saw a garden party being filmed out on the lawn of some big swell home. The ladies were all dressed so beautiful.

They were joined in California by Helen and Ted, Dad's sister and Mother's brother. Uncle Ted had a real job (bending pipe I think) and they lived in a real house in Compton. Their baby,

Kenneth, was born there, and some how or other earned money as a newborn "extra" in a number of movies. Mother took him to the set and was thrilled to meet some of the current "stars"…I remember one was heart throb, John Boles. We used to go to the beach with my Aunt Helen and Uncle Ted.

Things must have been looking up because at the close of this long letter she reports:

Barbara got some new shoes and she sure is crazy about them... black patent. Write to 2257 W. Pico, Los Angeles. That's the shop address. Barbara wrote you a letter:

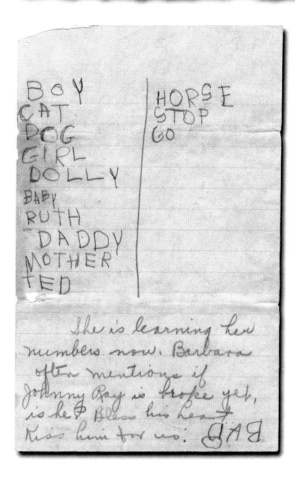

The reference in this letter "Barbara often mentions if Johnny Ray is broke yet, is he?" is testament to how important it was in this pre-Dr. Spock era to "break" kids. It was a sign of a good and conscientious mother to break (toilet train) a child at an early age. I was, of course, broken at a very early age.

And so ends the 8,000 mile journey from St. Louis to Los Angeles. A journey through mud, dust, unbearable heat, through the plains, the desert, the mountains, following the pipeline in vain and harvesting fruit for a pittance.

Did this experience help me shoulder
Vicissitudes as I grew older?

Well, yes
I guess.

Whether it did or not, my memories of Homeless on the Range bring a warm glow to my heart and the sound of our three voices as we sang, "Swing Low, Sweet Chariot, coming for to carry me home" echoes and re-echoes in my dreams.

EPILOGUE

Yes, eventually things did get better. They could not have gotten much worse.

My dad finally found work in St. Louis, and after several years of living marginally we were thrilled to rent a home with indoor plumbing. My years of walking to the outhouse in the dark of night remains one of my most lingering memories. I remember reciting the 23rd Psalm on many a dark night on my way to that smelly two-holer.

My parents prospered, as did many in this great nation, who never doubted that life would get better. When I was thirteen they were able to buy a home in the St. Louis suburb of Ferguson, where I attended high school and met my future husband, Don Margerum.

Don and I married, moved to California and had three wonderful children, Hugh, Amy and Doug. They are extraordinary people, and our lives are constantly enriched by them. We now live in Santa Barbara, the home of the free camping spot that years earlier Mom and Dad described as "sure was a nice place".

It is my fondest hope that HOMELESS ON THE RANGE, will live on as a tribute to my wonderful and courageous mother and father, Ruth and Hugh Barden.

BUFFALO GALS

As I was walking down the street
Down the street, down the street,
A pretty little gal I chanced to meet,
Oh, she was fair to see.

Chorus

Buffalo Gals, won't you come out tonight.
Come out tonight, come out tonight
Buffalo Gals won't you come out tonight
And dance by the light of the moon.

I stopped her and we had a talk,
Had a talk, had a talk,
Her feet took up the whole sidewalk
And left no room for me.

Chorus

I danced with a gal with a hole in her stockin',
And her heel kept a-knockin', and her toes kept a rockin'
I danced with a gal with a hole in her stockin'
And we danced by the light of the moon.

Chorus

SWING LOW, SWEET CHARIOT

Swing low, sweet chariot,
Comin' for to carry me home!

I looked over Jordan and what did I see,
Comin' for to carry me home!
A band of angels comin' after me,
Comin' for to carry me home!

Swing low, sweet chariot,
Comin' for to carry me home!

If you get there before I do,
Comin' for to carry me home,
Jess tell my friends that I'm acomin' too,
Comin' for to carry me home.

Swing low, sweet chariot,
Comin' for to carry me home!

I'm sometimes up and sometimes down,
Comin' for to carry me home,
But still my soul feels heavenly bound
Comin' for to carry me home!

OH, DEM GOLDEN SLIPPERS

Oh, dem golden slippers!
Oh, dem golden slippers!
Golden slippers I'm gwine to wear
Because dey look so neat.

Oh, dem golden slippers!
Oh, dem golden slippers!
Golden slippers I'se gwine to wear
To walk de golden street.

SO LONG! OO-LONG
(How Long You Gonna Be Gone)

Ming Toy loved a boy,
Happy little Japanee;
Oo-long was his name,
Set her heart a flame.
One day he say, "Soon I gotta go away;"
When he leave Ming Toy grieve;
Everybody hear her say:

"So long! Oo-long, how long you gonna be gone?
Your little Japanee,
Will be waiting underneath the bamboo tree;
So don't be too long,
Oo-long I'll long while you're away
Waiting for the day when you'll come back to me.
I'll sit and sigh, 'Neath the Oriental sky,
Each day that I am left a lone In Naki Saki.
So long! Oo-Long, How long you goin' to roam?
Please don't be too long
Oo-long, so long hurry back home."

CPSIA information can be obtained at www.ICGtesting.com
Printed in the USA
LVOW06s0038160414

381904LV00012B/392/P